Module 3

Working With Your QuickBooks® Items - Part 1

Introduction

Working and teaching hundreds of small business owners and bookkeepers throughout the years, I have learned that education is the key to success.

This material is for informational purposes only and is not intended to substitute for obtaining accounting, tax, or legal advice from a licensed professional for your particular situation. There is no liability or responsibility assumed for any errors or omissions in the content of this book, as federal and state laws and policies may change. The U.S. and Texas state tax advice contained in this book is not intended to be used for the purpose of avoiding penalties under federal or state law. Reasonable efforts have been made to furnish accurate and up-to-date information, however it is not warranted that it is accurate, complete, reliable, current, or error free. Information has been obtained from the Texas Workforce Commission, the Internal Revenue Service, the Social Security Administration, and the United States Department of Labor.

About the Author

Dwayne J. Briscoe is a Certified QuickBooks ProAdvisor® with over 10 years of experience supporting businesses and individuals who utilize QuickBooks®. Since Dwayne's work in teaching QuickBooks® for over 7 years, he has taught over 1,000 small business owners and bookkeepers through local area Small Business Development Centers, public and private instruction, and Brazosport College.

Working With Your QuickBooks® Items List - Part 1

Objectives

1.   Learn what the Items List is and the definitions of the eleven different types: Service, Inventory Part, Non-inventory Part, Inventory Assembly, Other Charge, Subtotal, Group, Discount, Payment, Sales Tax Item, and Sales Tax Group.

2.   Subitems and Units of Measure for each item.

3.   Performing searches and sorts in your Items List.

Objective 1 - Learn what the Items List is and the definitions of the eleven different types: Service, Inventory Part, Non-inventory Part, Inventory Assembly, Other Charge, Subtotal, Group, Discount, Payment, Sales Tax Item, and Sales Tax Group.

Retrieving the Sample Company File

We are going to use the sample company file (Rock Castle Construction) provided by QuickBooks® for the remainder of this module. To find the file, go to your start button on the bottom left-hand side, and when you click on it, you'll see a box that says *Search programs and files* with a magnifying glass next to it. It may look different depending upon the version of Windows® you're using on your computer.

The file that you're searching for is

sample_product-based business.qbw

When you've found this file, move your cursor over the file and double-click it. This will open your QuickBooks® software and the sample company file, Rock Castle Construction. There will be a window that appears noting that this is a sample file and click the blue OK button. When it opens, you'll see at the top, Sample Rock Castle Construction, which identifies your file.

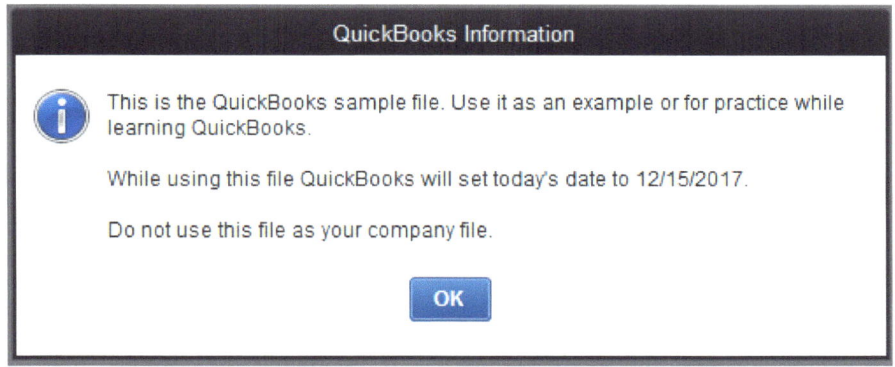

The Items List is what you will be selling as goods and services that you sell to customers tracked in the appropriate income account(s) and purchase from vendors that you will be tracking in the appropriate Cost of Goods Sold (COGS) account(s). There are special items for which you will be able to utilize further calculations, which include: subtotals, discounts, and sales tax. You can edit each Item but if it is used in at least one transaction, you cannot delete it unless you move the transaction(s) to another Item.

You can reach the Items List by either using your drop-down menu from List on the Menu Bar, or choosing the Items & Services icon on your Home Page, located in the Company section.

Figure 1

Figure 2

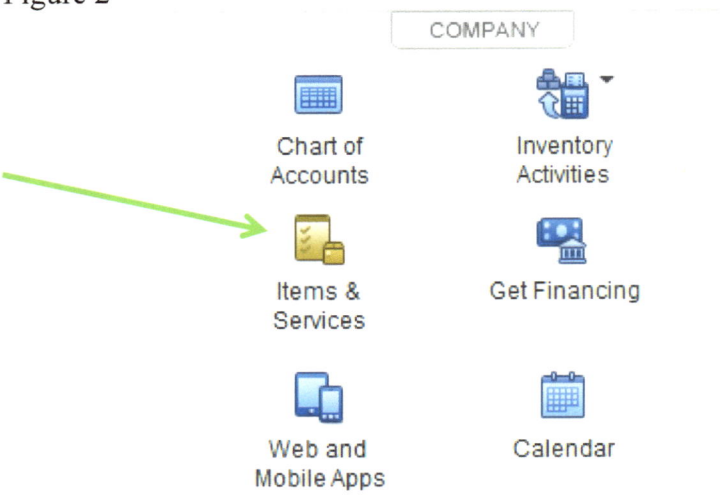

When you open up your Items List, you will need to populate your items based upon each product, inventory parts, non-inventory parts, services, sales tax, other charges, and discounts. If your business collects sales tax, you must make sure that the Sales Tax Preferences section is turned on and your tax preferences are set up. If you sell Inventory, you must make sure that your Items & Inventory section is turned on and set up.

You have 3 options of adding a new Item.

1. To choose a new Item, in the bottom left-hand side of your screen, you will see the icon Item. Choose the drop-down arrow, and click on New.

2. To choose a new Item, you have a short-cut key, Ctrl-N you can use while you are in the Items List screen.

3. To choose a new Item, click on Edit from the menu bar and choose New while you are in the Items List.

File   Edit   View

When you add a new Item, you will then determine what its "Type" is below from the drop-down menu:

Notes / Custom Fields / Spelling

Located on the right-hand side of each item you open, you will have 3 additional options of use for assistance in preparing and revising your Item: Notes, Custom Fields, and Spelling.

Notes refers to allowing you to set up specific reminders , information, To Do items, etc. as it is noted in other areas of QuickBooks®.

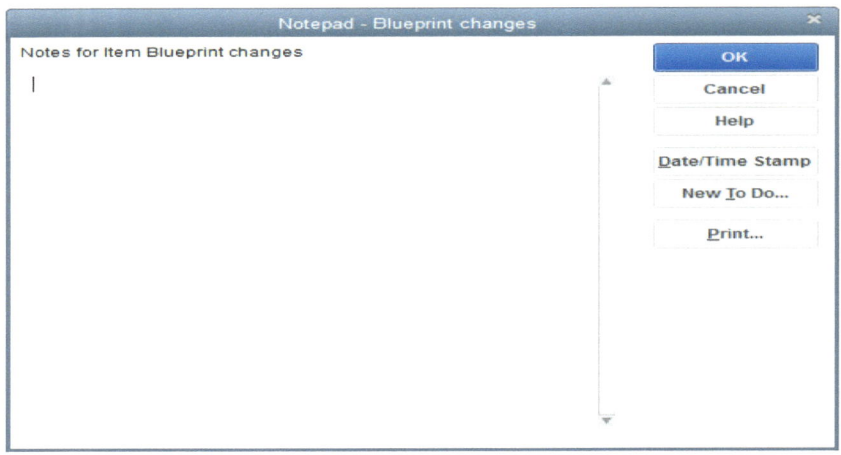

Custom Fields is a similar option such as Define Fields available in the Customer, Vendor, and Employee Centers. You can add, change, edit, and delete these fields, however you are limited to only four fields total.

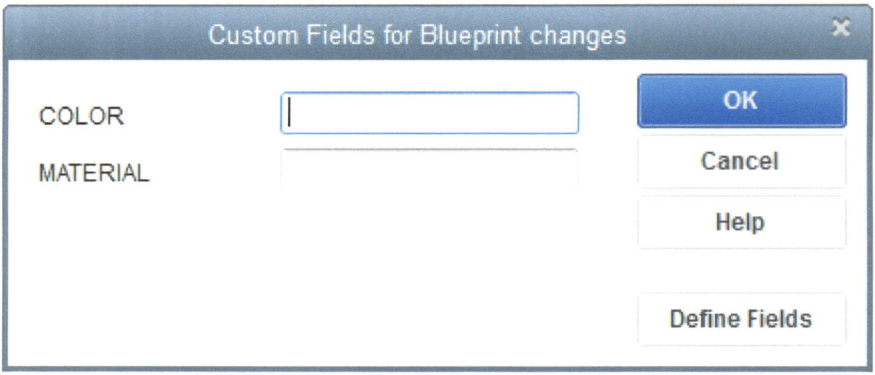

Spelling is giving you the option of running a spell check on each item's information.

Service – Use for services you charge for or purchase, like specialized labor, consulting hours, or professional fees; something that is not tangible but is labor-related.

When the Service Item has been saved, you CANNOT change it to another Item Type, because the box is shaded. If it is NOT shaded, then you have a limited amount of options to change the Type.

- *Item Name/Number* should be relevant to describing the Service.

- the box for *This service is used in assemblies or is performed by a subcontractor or partner* is checked which allows you to set up a Purchase section and a Sales section; if the box is unchecked, you will only have a Sales Section

- *Description on Purchase Transactions* is what information that's relayed to vendors

- *Description on Sales Transactions* is what information that's relayed to customers

- *Cost* refers to your cost being charged by your vendor; this does not need to be completed and can be left at 0.00 if the price will change on a regular basis

- *Sales Price* refers your cost being charged to your customer; this does not need to be completed and can be left at 0.00 if the price will change on a regular basis

- *Expenses Account* refers to what account will be charged when you attach a bill to this Service Item, i.e. expense account or COGS account

- *Tax Code* refers to whether the Service item is either taxable or nontaxable

- *Preferred Vendor* refers to a specific vendor you purchase this service from

- *Income Account* refers to what account will be charged when you charge a customer to this Service Item

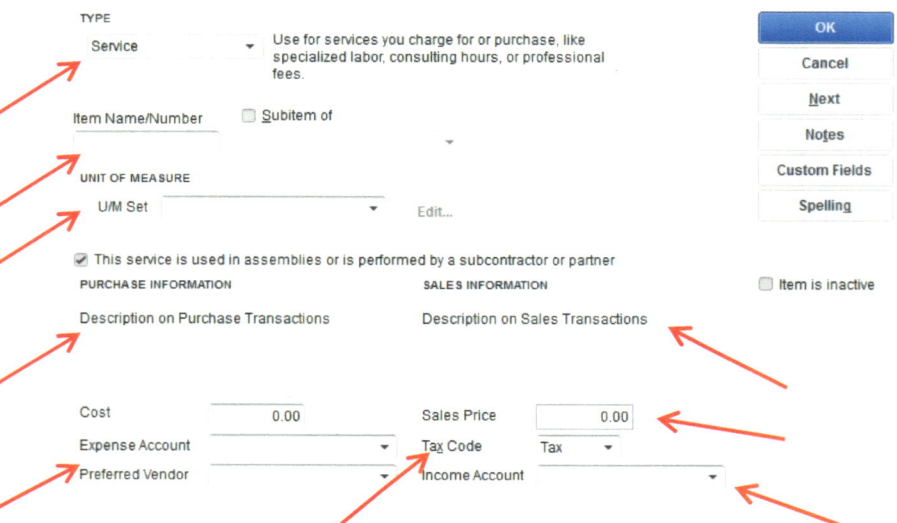

When you review the information above, choose the Cancel button in the Item window, which is located in the top right-side of the window to go out of the screen above.

While the List is still open, scroll down and highlight the word Carpet and double-click it.

⋄ Labor	
⋄ Removal	Removal labor
⋄ Repairs	Repair work
⋄ Subs	Subcontracted services
⋄ Carpet	Install carpeting
⋄ Drywall	Install drywall
⋄ Duct Work	Heating & Air Conditioning Duct Work
⋄ Electrical	Electrical work

The following window appears. In this example, you see that the Item Name/Number is Carpet. It is a "Subitem of" which will be discussed in Objective 4.

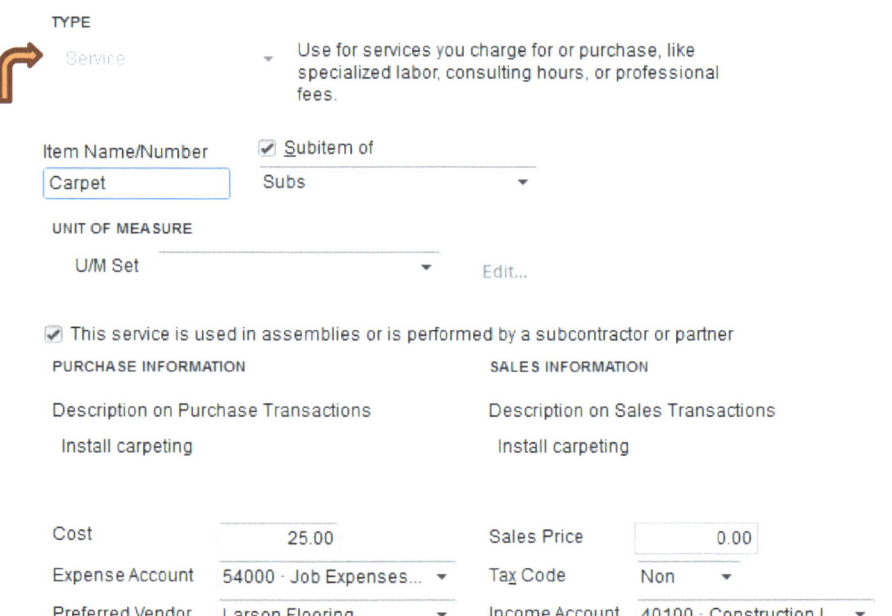

The box for "This service is…" has been checked and separated out to differentiate the Purchase and Sales Transactions. You will see that the Expense Account falls under the COGS account section as a default, in the sample company file. This is considered the largest expense of the Profit and Loss Statement because it's what it is sold by the company and NOT an overhead expense. Any products or services that a company sells should always be coded to the COGS section of your Chart of Accounts and not classified to an expense account.

Account	Type
◦ 50100 · Cost of Goods Sold	Cost of Goods Sold
◦ 54000 · Job Expenses	Cost of Goods Sold
◦ 54100 · Bond Expense	Cost of Goods Sold
◦ 54200 · Equipment Rental	Cost of Goods Sold
◦ 54300 · Job Materials	Cost of Goods Sold
◦ 54400 · Permits and Licenses	Cost of Goods Sold
◦ 54500 · Subcontractors	Cost of Goods Sold
◦ 54520 · Freight & Delivery	Cost of Goods Sold
◦ 54599 · Less Discounts Taken	Cost of Goods Sold

You will see that the Income Account falls under the Income account section, as noted below from the Chart of Accounts, in the sample company file. This is considered the revenue of the Profit and Loss Statement because it's what it is received from the sales of your service and products by the company.

Account	Type
◦ 40100 · Construction Income	Income
◦ 40110 · Design Income	Income
◦ 40120 · Equipment Rental Income	Income
◦ 40130 · Labor Income	Income
◦ 40140 · Materials Income	Income
◦ 40150 · Subcontracted Labor Income	Income
◦ 40199 · Less Discounts given	Income
◦ 40500 · Reimbursement Income	Income
◦ 40510 · Mileage Income	Income
◦ 40520 · Permit Reimbursement Income	Income
◦ 40530 · Reimbursed Freight & Delivery	Income

When you review the information above, choose the Cancel button in the Item window, which is located in the top right-side of the window.

While the List is open, scroll down and highlight the item Cabinet Pulls and double-click it.

◇ Cabinets	Cabinets	Inventory Part
◇ Cabinet Pulls	Cabinet Pulls	Inventory Part
◇ Light Pine	Light pine kitchen cabinet wall unit	Inventory Part

Inventory Part – Used for goods you purchase, track as inventory, and resell.

When the Inventory Part Item has been saved, you can only change it to Inventory Assembly.

- *Item Name/Number* should be relevant to describing the Inventory Part.

  Please note that there is no *This service is used in assemblies or is performed by a subcontractor or partner* option box to check for Inventory Parts because it is required to have a separate Purchase and Sales section

- *Description on Purchase Transactions* is what information that's relayed to vendors

- *Description on Sales Transactions* is what information that's relayed to customers

- *Cost* refers to your cost being charged by your vendor; this does not need to be completed and can be left at 0.00 if the price will change on a regular basis; however upon receipt of inventory, you will be asked if you want to change the price to determine your profit margins

- *Sales Price* refers your cost being charged to your customer; this does not need to be completed and can be left at 0.00 if the price will change on a regular basis; however upon the sale of inventory, you will be asked if you want to change the price to determine your profit margins
- *COGS Account* refers to what account will be charged when you attach a bill to this Inventory Part

- *Tax Code* refers to whether the Inventory Part item is either taxable or nontaxable

- *Preferred Vendor* refers to a specific vendor you purchase this service from

- *Income Account* refers to what account will be charged when you charge a customer to this Service Item

- *Inventory Information* has multiple sections:

  - *Asset Account* refers to the Inventory Asset account where the value of your inventory will be tracked; you can have multiple Inventory Asset accounts if it's a necessity instead of having just one major account

  - *Reorder Point* refers to the base amount that this particular Inventory Part should have in stock at all times determined by your inventory control manager

  - *On Hand* refers to the current amount of items in stock according to your file

  - *Total Value* refers to the current dollar value of items in stock according to your file

  - *As of* will demonstrate the date according to your file

When you review the information above, choose the Cancel button in the Item window, which is located in the top right-side of the window.

While the List is open, scroll down and highlight the item Trim Lumber and double-click it.

◇ Lumber	Lumber	Non-inventory Part
◇ Trim	Trim lumber	Non-inventory Part
◇ Decking	Decking lumber	Non-inventory Part
◇ Rough	Rough lumber	Non-inventory Part

<u>Non-inventory Part</u> – Use for goods you buy but don't track materials for a specific job that you charge back to the customer.

When the Non-inventory Part Item has been saved, you can only change it to: Service, Inventory Part, or Other Charge.

- *Item Name/Number* should be relevant to describing the Non-inventory Part.

- the box for *This service is used in assemblies or is performed by a subcontractor or partner* is checked which allows you to set up a Purchase section and a Sales section; if the box is unchecked, you will only have a Sales Section

- *Description on Purchase Transactions* is what information that's relayed to vendors

- *Description on Sales Transactions* is what information that's relayed to customers

- *Cost* refers to your cost being charged by your vendor; this does not need to be completed and can be left at 0.00 if the price will change on a regular basis; however upon receipt of inventory, you will be asked if you want to change the price to determine your profit margins

- *Sales Price* refers your cost being charged to your customer; this does not need to be completed and can be left at 0.00 if the price will change on a regular basis; however upon the sale of inventory, you will be asked if you want to change the price to determine your profit margins

- *Expense Account* refers to what account will be charged when you attach a bill to this Non-inventory Part

- *Tax Code* refers to whether the Non-inventory Part item is either taxable or nontaxable

- *Preferred Vendor* refers to a specific vendor you purchase this Non-inventory Part from

- *Income Account* refers to what account will be charged when you charge a customer to this Non-inventory Part

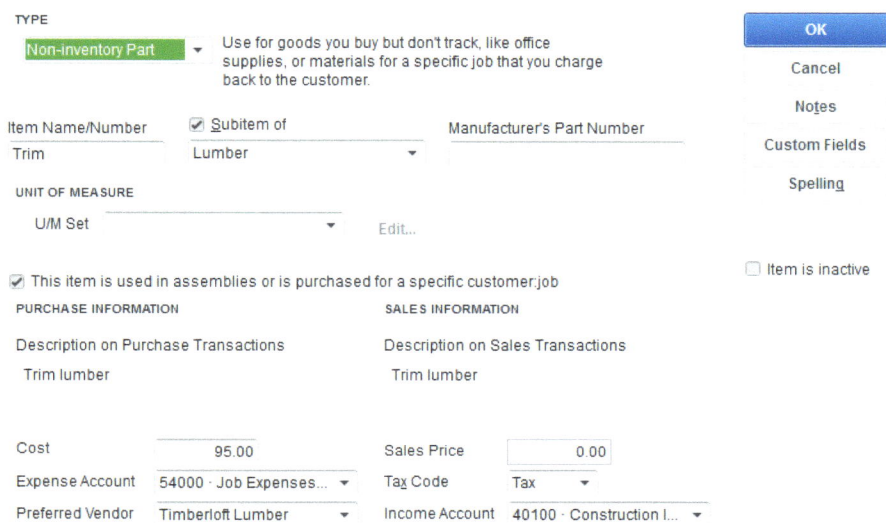

TYPE

Non-inventory Part ▾   Use for goods you buy but don't track, like office
                        supplies, or materials for a specific job that you charge
                        back to the customer.

Item Name/Number   ☑ Subitem of   Manufacturer's Part Number

Trim   Lumber   ▾

UNIT OF MEASURE

U/M Set   ▾   Edit...

☑ This item is used in assemblies or is purchased for a specific customer:job

PURCHASE INFORMATION   SALES INFORMATION

Description on Purchase Transactions   Description on Sales Transactions

Trim lumber   Trim lumber

Cost   95.00   Sales Price   0.00

Expense Account   54000 · Job Expenses... ▾   Tax Code   Tax ▾

Preferred Vendor   Timberloft Lumber   ▾   Income Account 40100 · Construction I... ▾

OK

Cancel

Notes

Custom Fields

Spelling

☐ Item is inactive

When you review the information above, choose the Cancel button in the Item window, which is located in the top right-side of the window.

While the List is open, scroll down and highlight the item Interior Door Kit and double-click it.

◆ Interior Door kit   complete Interior door   Inventory Assembly

Inventory Assembly – Use for goods you buy but don't track materials for a specific job that you charge back to the customer.

When the Inventory Assembly Item has been saved, you CANNOT change it to another Item Type, because the box is shaded.

- *Item Name/Number* should be relevant to describing the Inventory Assembly Item.

- the box for *I purchase this assembly from a vendor* is checked which allows you to set up a Purchase section and a Sales section; if the box is unchecked, you will only have a Sales Section

- *Description on Purchase Transactions* is what information that's relayed to vendors

- *Description on Sales Transactions* is what information that's relayed to customers

- *Cost* refers to your cost being charged by your vendor; this does not need to be completed and can be left at 0.00 if the price will change on a regular basis; however upon receipt of inventory, you will be asked if you want to change the price to determine your profit margins

- *Sales Price* refers your cost being charged to your customer; this does not need to be completed and can be left at 0.00 if the price will change on a regular basis; however upon the sale of inventory, you will be asked if you want to change the price to determine your profit margins

- *COGS Account* refers to what account will be charged when you attach a bill to this Inventory Assembly

- *Tax Code* refers to whether the Inventory Assembly item is either taxable or nontaxable

- *Preferred Vendor* refers to a specific vendor you purchase this service from

- *Income Account* refers to what account will be charged when you charge a customer to this Inventory Assembly Item

- *Bill of Materials* allows you to add any of the following items: Inventory Part, Non-inventory Part, Service, another Inventory Assembly, or Other Charge

  - When you click on each line, you will see a drop-down menu which will allow you choose any of the items you have set up from the different types.

- *Inventory Information* has multiple sections:

  - *Asset Account* refers to the Inventory Asset account where the value of your inventory will be tracked; you can have multiple Inventory Asset accounts if it's a necessity instead of having just one major account

  - *Build Point* refers to the base amount that this particular Inventory Assembly should have in stock at all times

  - *On Hand* refers to the current amount of items in stock according to your file

  - *Total Value* refers to the current dollar value of items in stock according to your file

  - *On Sales Order* will demonstrate the amount being held for sales

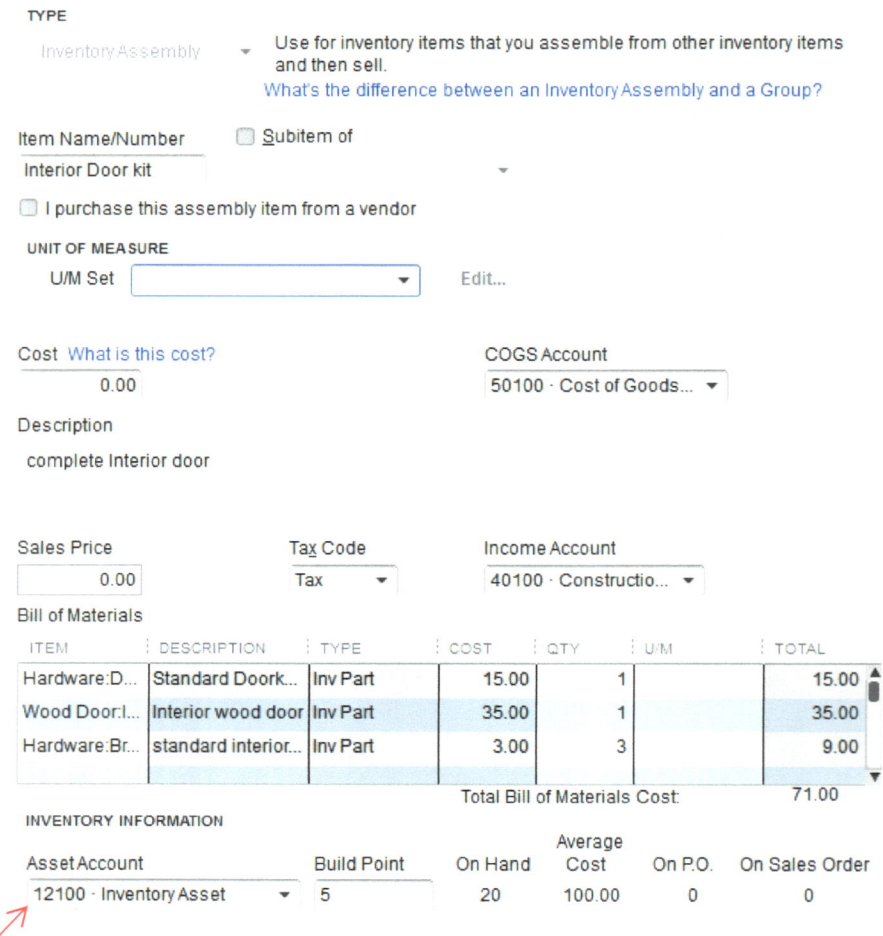

TYPE

Inventory Assembly ▾ Use for inventory items that you assemble from other inventory items and then sell.
What's the difference between an Inventory Assembly and a Group?

Item Name/Number ☐ Subitem of

Interior Door kit ▾

☐ I purchase this assembly item from a vendor

UNIT OF MEASURE

U/M Set ▾ Edit...

Cost What is this cost?   COGS Account

0.00   50100 · Cost of Goods... ▾

Description

complete Interior door

Sales Price	Tax Code	Income Account
0.00	Tax ▾	40100 · Constructio... ▾

Bill of Materials

ITEM	DESCRIPTION	TYPE	COST	QTY	U/M	TOTAL
Hardware:D...	Standard Doork...	Inv Part	15.00	1		15.00
Wood Door:I...	Interior wood door	Inv Part	35.00	1		35.00
Hardware:Br...	standard interior...	Inv Part	3.00	3		9.00

Total Bill of Materials Cost: 71.00

INVENTORY INFORMATION

Asset Account	Build Point	On Hand	Average Cost	On P.O.	On Sales Order
12100 · Inventory Asset ▾	5	20	100.00	0	0

When you review the information above, choose the Cancel button in the Item window, which is located in the top right-side of the window.

While the List is open, scroll down and highlight the item Interior Delivery Charge and double-click it.

◈ Freight Reimb...	Freight and Delivery Reimbursement	Other Charge
◈ Deposit		Other Charge
◈ Bad debt	Bad debt or write-off amounts	Other Charge
◈ Delivery Charg...	Freight & Delivery	Other Charge
◈ Equip Rental	Equipment Rental	Other Charge

<u>Other Charge</u> – Used for miscellaneous labor, material, or part charges, such as delivery charges, setup fees, and service charges.

When the Other Charge item has been saved, you can only change it to: Service, Inventory Part, Inventory Assembly, or Non-inventory Part.

- *Item Name/Number* should be relevant to describing the Other Charge.

- the box for *This item is used in assemblies or is a reimbursable charge* is checked which allows you to set up a Purchase section and a Sales section; if the box is unchecked, you will only have a Sales Section

- *Description on Purchase Transactions* is what information that's relayed to vendors

- *Description on Sales Transactions* is what information that's relayed to customers

- *Cost* refers to your cost being charged by your vendor; this does not need to be completed and can be left at 0.00 if the price will change on a regular basis; however upon receipt of inventory, you will be asked if you want to change the price to determine your profit margins

- *Sales Price* refers your cost being charged to your customer; this does not need to be completed and can be left at 0.00 if the price will change on a regular basis; however upon the sale of inventory, you will be asked if you want to change the price to determine your profit margins

- *Expense Account* refers to what account will be charged when you attach a bill to this Other Charge; this is usually a COGS account because you are working with the Items List but it can also be an overhead expense account

- *Tax Code* refers to whether the Other Charge item is either taxable or nontaxable

- *Preferred Vendor* refers to a specific vendor you purchase this Other Charge from

- *Income Account* refers to what account will be charged when you charge a customer to this Other Charge

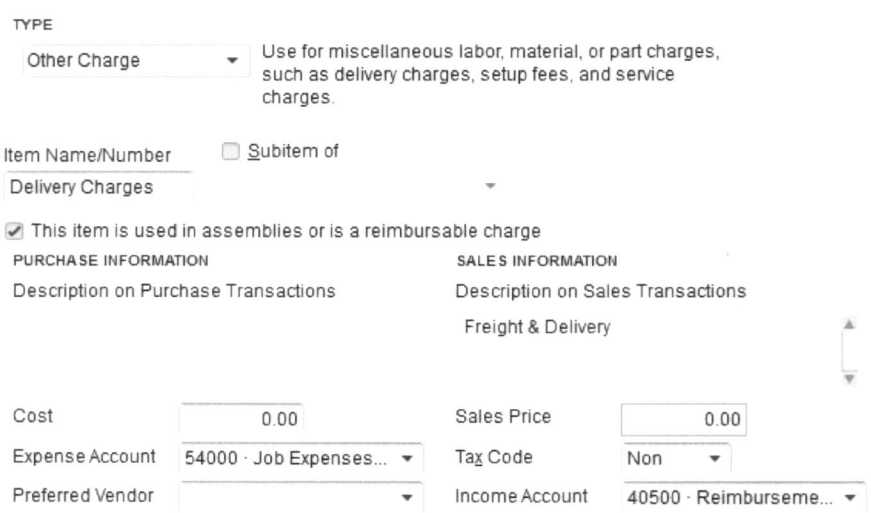

When you review the information above, choose the Cancel button in the Item window, which is located in the top right-side of the window.

While the List is open, scroll down and highlight the item Subtotal and double-click it.

Subtotal – Use to total all items above it on a form, up to the last subtotal. It is useful for applying a percentage discount or surcharge to many items.

When the Subtotal item has been saved, you CANNOT change it to another Item Type, because the box is shaded.

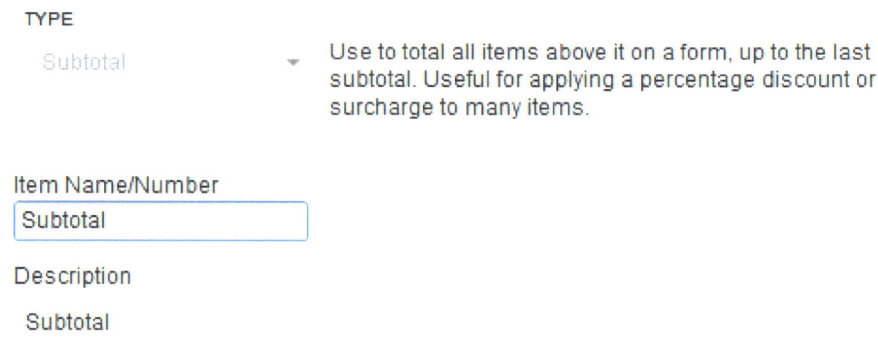

When you review the information above, choose the Cancel button in the Item window, which is located in the top right-side of the window.

While the List is open, scroll down and highlight the item A1 Custom Storage and double-click.

⬦ A1 Custom Sto...	Custom Storage Building - Model A1	Group
⬦ A2 Custom Sto...	Custom Storage Building - Model A2	Group
⬦ A3 Custom Sto...	Custom Storage Building - model A3	Group
⬦ Door set	Exterior door and hardware set	Group
⬦ Reimb Group	Time and materials	Group
⬦ Room Addition/...	Project Total	Group

Group – Used for miscellaneous labor, material, or part charges, such as delivery charges, setup fees, and service charges.

When the Group item has been saved, you CANNOT change it to another Item Type, because the box is shaded.

- *Group Name/Number* should be relevant to describing the Group.

- *Description* is what information that's relayed to customers

- the box for *Print items in group* is checked which allows you to print each line item in your group under the Group Name/Number; if the box is unchecked, you will only have the Group Name/Number print

- your Group item allows you to add any of the following items: Inventory Part, Non-inventory Part, Service, another Inventory Assembly, or Other Charge

  - When you click on each line, you will see a drop-down menu which will allow you choose any of the items you have set up from the different types.

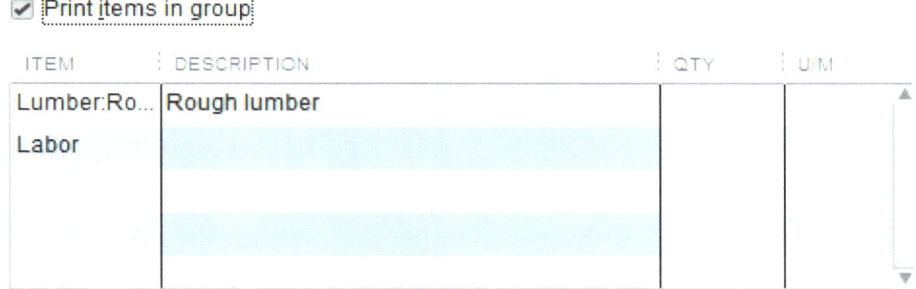

TYPE

Group ⌄   Use to quickly enter a group of individual items on an invoice.

What's the difference between a Group and an Inventory Assembly?

Group Name/Number

A1 Custom Storage Shed

Description

Custom Storage Building - Model A1

☑ Print items in group

ITEM	DESCRIPTION	QTY	U/M
Lumber:Ro...	Rough lumber		
Labor			

What's the difference between Group and inventory Assembly Items?

Group items and inventory assembly items are similar in that they both let you record a group of items as a single entry on purchase or sales forms, but they also have some important differences.

- Group items are useful for quickly entering a group of individual items that you often purchase or sell together.

  Assembly items let you combine inventory items and assembly costs into new, separately trackable items that represent the finished goods you produce and sell.

The following table compares group and assembly items to help you decide which item type is appropriate for your situation.

Group item	Inventory assembly item
Can include any item type except other groups.	Can contain any of the following item types: service, inventory part, inventory assembly, noninventory part, other charge. Notice that you can include other inventory assemblies (subassemblies) within an inventory assembly.
Enables you to print on sales forms the individual items contained in the group.	Prints only the assembly name, not component part names, on sales forms.
No reports available specifically for groups.	Appears after inventory part items on standard inventory reports; Pending Builds report lists assembly builds in the pending state.
Quantity on hand of each item included in the group is adjusted in inventory at the time of sale.	Quantity on hand of component items is adjusted in inventory when the assembly is built.
Sales tax is calculated by individual items included in the sales tax group item.	One sales tax code applies to the entire assembly, even if component item sales tax codes differ.
Cannot be included in another group item (nested) or in an inventory assembly item.	Can be included (nested) in other inventory assembly items and included in group items.
For groups of inventory parts, QuickBooks tracks inventory of items in the group, not the group itself.	QuickBooks tracks assembly items in inventory.

Price of a group item is the sum of the items in the group (although you can include an item in the group for a discount or additional charge to adjust the simple sum calculation).	Price of an assembly item can be anything you specify.
Can include both taxable and nontaxable items.	Must be designated as either taxable or nontaxable.

When you review the information above, choose the Cancel button in the Item window, which is located in the top right-side of the window.

While the List is open, scroll down and highlight the item Discount and double-click it.

Discount – Use to subtract a percentage or fixed amount from a total or subtotal. Do not use this item type for an early payment discount, because its purpose is to demonstrate the discount before payment is received.

This is a similar option to setting up a Price Level for your customers however this is directly applied on the Sales Receipt and Invoice.

When the Discount item has been saved, you CANNOT change it to another Item Type, because the box is shaded.

- *Discount* should be relevant to describing the Discount.

- *Description* is what information that's relayed to customers

- *Amount or %* refers to a specific dollar figure ($0.00) that you will be deducting from the invoice or sales receipt, or a particular percentage (5.0%) deducted from the invoice or sales receipt. Remember that when you do a percentage amount, you must have .0% in front of the amount so you have a whole number, i.e. 5%, 10%, 20%, etc.

- *Account* refers to what account will be charged when you give the discounts. In the sample company, they have an Income account called "Less Discounts Given" which you can set up into your own chart of accounts.

- *Tax Code* refers to whether the discount is taken before or after the sales tax. If you choose "Non" it will be taken after the sales tax has been applied. If you choose "Tax" it will be taken before the sales tax has been applied. If you want certain customers to receive a discount before sales tax and after sales tax, you need to set up two separate Discount items and differentiate them in the Discount information box.

When you review the information above, choose the Cancel button in the Item window, which is located in the top right-side of the window.
While the List is open, scroll down and highlight the item Prepayment and double-click it.

⬦ Pre-Payment		Payment
⬦ Payment	Down payment received	Payment

Payment – Use to record a partial payment at the time of the sale. It reduces the amount owed on an invoice.

When the Payment item has been saved, you CANNOT change it to another Item Type, because the box is shaded.

- *Item Name/Number* should be relevant to describing the Payment.

- *Description* is what information that's relayed to customers

- *Payment Method* is chosen to what form of payment is received from the drop down menu: Cash, Check, American Express, Discover Card, MasterCard, Visa, Barter, E-check. You have the option of adding additional payment methods by choosing *<Add New>* at the top of the drop-down menu.

- *Group with other undeposited funds* gives you the option of having these payments added to the Undeposited Funds account ("collects the records of all of your received amounts into one account; from there, you will choose the payments made for that particular day and condense it into one deposit, which will allow you to perform your bank reconciliation easier") or *Deposit To* a specific bank, accounts receivable, or other current asset account set up in your Chart of Accounts that is deposited directly as a single payment.

Setting Up Sales Tax Item(s)

When setting up the Sales Tax Item(s) in your Items List, you must set up the Sales Tax Tab in your Company Preferences under the Edit drop-down menu. If you are unsure if you should be charging sales tax, check with your State Comptroller. In setting up the Sales Tax Item, you will be required to develop the most common sales tax item, which could be labeled as Texas State or something similar.

When you go into Edit > Preferences > Sales Tax, the following window opens. You must be in the Company Preferences section in order to make changes to your Sales Tax options.

1. If you charge sales tax, you must choose yes.

My Preferences	Company Preferences

Do you charge sales tax? ⦿ Yes ○ No

SET UP SALES TAX ITEM

Add a sales tax item for each county, district, parish, etc. where you collect sales tax.   Show Examples

Your most common sales tax item

Add sales tax item...	Texas State ▾

ASSIGN SALES TAX CODES

Sales tax codes determine if the items you sell are taxable or non-taxable.

Taxable item code Tax ▾   Non-taxable item code Non ▾

☑ Identify taxable amounts as "T" for "Taxable" when printing

WHEN DO YOU OWE SALES TAX?

○ As of invoice date (Accrual Basis)
⦿ Upon receipt of payment (Cash Basis)

WHEN DO YOU PAY SALES TAX?

⦿ Monthly
○ Quarterly
○ Annually

2. When completing the "Assign Tax Codes" you will default to what appears above.

3. "When do you owe sales tax" is determined by whether or not you file your taxes on a cash or accrual basis.

4. "When do you pay sales tax" is determined by the schedule after receiving your sales tax permit from your State Comptroller."

5. When you choose "Add Sales Tax Item" the following window appears. From there you must choose "Sales Tax Item" for your "Type."

6. You type your "Sales Tax Name" which will be the governmental entity you are responsible to pay, which is limited to 14 characters.

7. You type your "Description," which will be much more detailed than your "Sales Tax Name."

8. You type your "Tax Rate" for the governmental entity you are responsible to pay.

9. You type the "Tax Agency" that is responsible for collecting your sales tax.

When you select Sales Tax Item, it will ask you for the Sales Tax Name and the tax rate you are charging for. If you are located in a brick & mortar single location where you sell taxable items and services only at that location, you utilize one sales tax amount for its location.

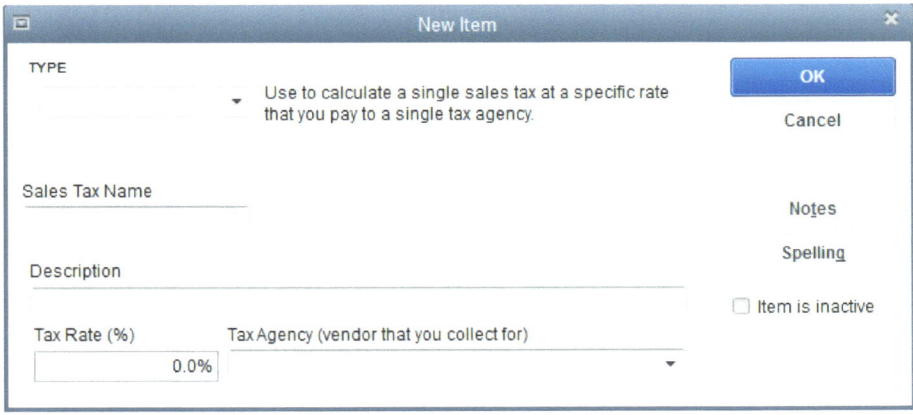

If you sell in multiple locations or perform taxable services in different locations, you must set up a different Sales Tax Item for each location based upon the area's physical location. The following link is for the Texas State Comptroller's office web site in this example.

https://ourcpa.cpa.state.tx.us/atj/addresslookup.jsp

In the example below, we typed in State of Texas for the Name, "Sales Tax" will automatically be defaulted in the Description and "State of Texas" was added, the state rate of 6.25%, and then the governmental entity responsible for collections is the Texas State Comptroller.

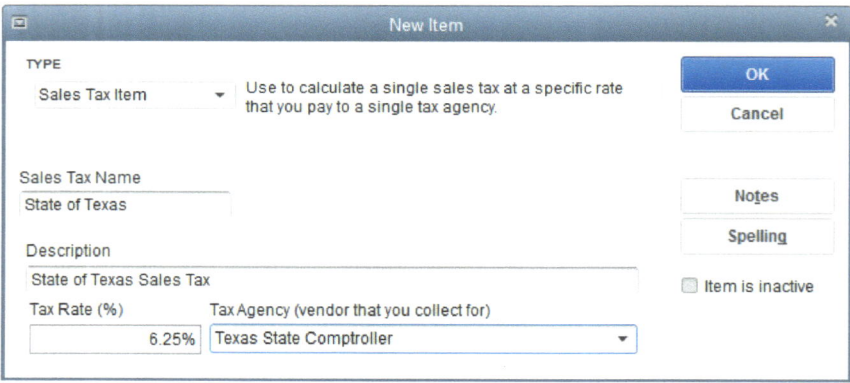

Because "Texas State Comptroller" was not already set up in the Vendor List, the following window will appear and ask you to either choose "Quick Add" which ONLY adds the name. If you choose "Set Up" then you can enter the full information, such as address, telephone number, etc. and then "Cancel" will not record any information.

The "Notes" and the "Spelling" options on the left side of the New Item window allows you to add additional notes to this particular item, as well as check the spelling for what you've typed. You also have the option of making the Item inactive.

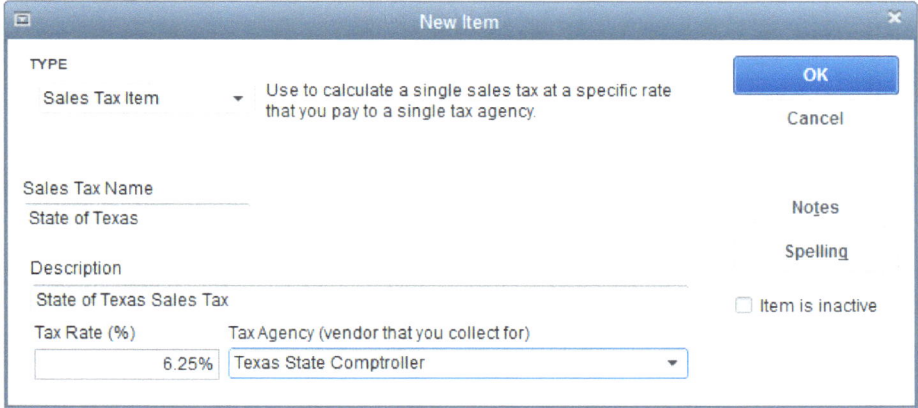

Because virtually every physical location in the United States has multiple tax entities, you must therefore assign each entity its own tax rate and set up a separate taxable item. From the taxable items, you will then develop a Sales Tax Item Group.

In the example below, it was noted that for 500 College Drive, Lake Jackson, Texas, there are three separate state governmental entities which sales tax must be collected for. There is County, City, and State.

As the State Tax Item has already been set up, you will use the same procedures for the County and City Tax Items. The Texas State Comptroller's Office collects and distributes all sales tax monies they will also be listed as the default Tax Agency. It is important to make sure that all entities are listed and set-up properly in QuickBooks® in the event of a sales tax audit and your file is requested as part of that process.

TYPE

Sales Tax Item   ▼   Use to calculate a single sales tax at a specific rate that you pay to a single tax agency.

Sales Tax Name

Brazoria

Description

Brazoria Sales Tax

Tax Rate (%)   Tax Agency (vendor that you collect for)

0.5%   Texas State Comptroller   ▼

Sales Tax Item ▾   Use to calculate a single sales tax at a specific rate that you pay to a single tax agency.

Sales Tax Name

Clute

Description

Clute Sales Tax

Tax Rate (%)	Tax Agency (vendor that you collect for)	
1.5%	Texas State Comptroller	▾

When you have completed all three jurisdictions, you will complete it with a Sales Tax Group. This gives you the total state tax payable of 8.25% (the maximum allowable by law in Texas) if your physical location is 500 College Drive. If you perform sales taxable services or sell your products at various locations, such as craft fairs or flea markets, trade shows, you must set up a similar Tax Group for each location. Each state has a maximum amount of sales tax it collects, so you must make sure that you are not collecting more than the maximum.

Exercises

1.   Which field isn't available in each Item > Edit screen?

      a. Spelling
      b. New
      c. Custom Field
      d. Notes

2.   Used to record a partial payment at the time of the sale.

      a. Discount
      b. Deposit
      c. Payment

3.   You can set up sales tax groups without setting up your sales tax items in Edit > Preferences section.

    a. True
    b. False

4.   Group items let you combine inventory items and assembly costs into new, separately trackable items that represent the finished goods you produce and sell.

    a. True
    b. False

5.   Assembly items are useful for quickly entering a group of individual items that you often purchase or sell together.

    a. True
    b. False

6.   When the Inventory Assembly Item has been saved, you CANNOT change it to another Item Type, because the box is shaded.

    a. True
    b. False

7.   What item refers to the base amount an Inventory Part should have in stock at all times?

    a. Expense Account
    b. COGS Account
    c. Inventory account
    d. Reorder Point

Objective 2 - Subitems and Units of Measure

Subitems

As it's an option throughout a number of areas within QuickBooks, you can also develop Subitems in the Items List. The purpose of creating subitems is that it allows a user to have more detailed and specific services, inventory parts, etc. and allows more detailed financial reporting measures.

As an example within the sample company file of Rockcastle Construction, in the Items List you see Subs as the "parent," but there's an additional nine subitems below it. The financial reporting can be broken down by sub item or Subs as the parent.

Subs	Subcontracted services
Carpet	Install carpeting
Drywall	Install drywall
Duct Work	Heating & Air Conditioning Duct Work
Electrical	Electrical work
Insulating	Install insulation
Metal Wrk	Metal Work
Painting	Painting
Plumbing	Plumbing
Roofing	Roofing

When adding a Subitem, you will develop a "New" Item by using the shortcut key Ctrl-N, and then a new window will appear. We will be adding a new subitem for Subs, so for Type we will use the drop-down menu and choose Service. Add the following information to the Subitem:

Item Name/Number – type in "Carpenter"

Subitem of – check this box

Subitem of – from the drop-down menu, choose Subs

This item is used in assemblies or is a reimbursable charge – check this box

Description on Purchase Transactions – type in "Framing work" and when you hit Tab the information will appear in *Description on Sales Transactions*

Cost – leave at 0.00 because this is a Service Item so amounts will vary

Expense Account – type in 54500, which is Subcontractors COGS, a subaccount of Job Expenses

Preferred Vendor – leave this blank

Sales Price – leave at 0.00 because this is a Service Item so amounts will vary

Tax Code – set as Non

Income Account – type in 40150, which is Subcontracted Labor Income, a subaccount of Construction Income

When this new Subitem is completed, click the OK button and review your Subs section.

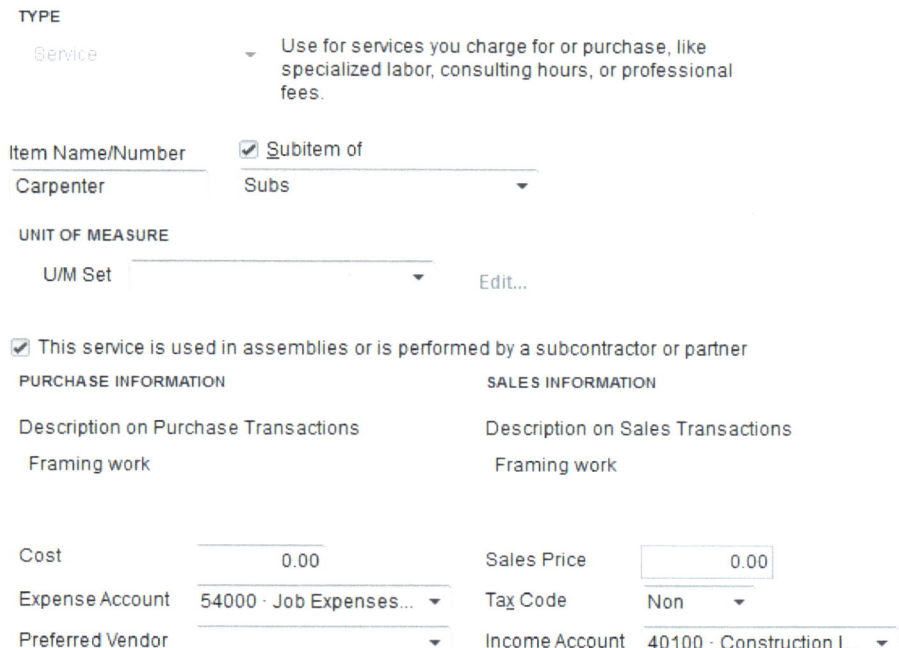

TYPE

Service   Use for services you charge for or purchase, like specialized labor, consulting hours, or professional fees.

Item Name/Number   ☑ Subitem of

Carpenter   Subs

UNIT OF MEASURE

U/M Set   Edit...

☑ This service is used in assemblies or is performed by a subcontractor or partner

PURCHASE INFORMATION   SALES INFORMATION

Description on Purchase Transactions   Description on Sales Transactions

Framing work   Framing work

Cost	0.00	Sales Price	0.00
Expense Account	54000 · Job Expenses...	Tax Code	Non
Preferred Vendor		Income Account	40100 · Construction I...

You will see that the Carpenter Subitem is under the parent Subs.

◇ Subs	Subcontracted services
◇ Carpenter	Framing work
◇ Carpet	Install carpeting
◇ Drywall	Install drywall

Units of Measure

When you need to add Units of Measure to an Item or Subitem, you must determine what the unit of measure is that you're going to be billing the customer and being billed by the vendor. When you open up the Subitem – Carpenter, you will see the Unit of Measure section.

From the U/M Set, use the drop-down menu and you will see the only Unit of Measure is "Each to *Case/Doz:ea*. Because Carpenters price jobs based upon a square foot basis, we will need to add a new measurement. From the drop-down menu, choose <Add New>. The following window appears.

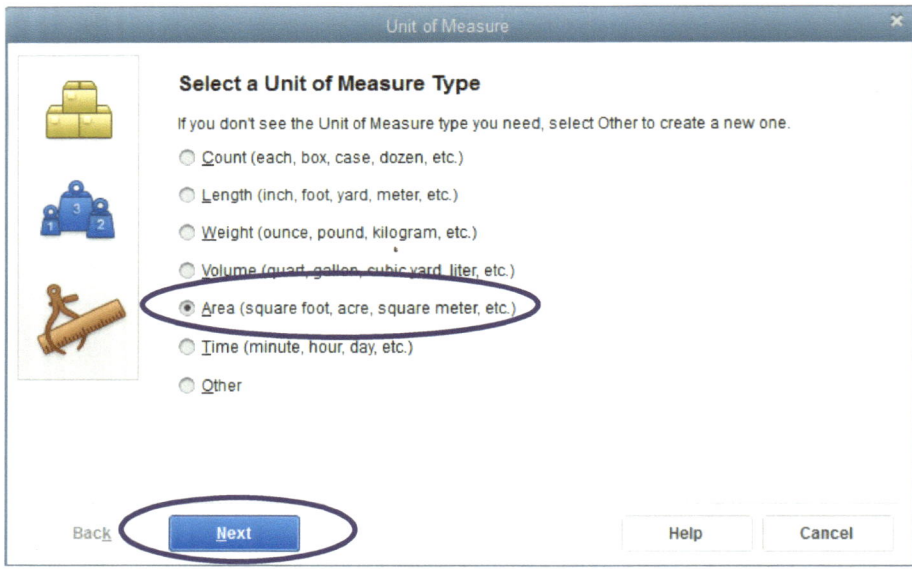

You have 7 different types of Unit of Measure. For our Carpenter, we will choose *Area*, which includes: square foot, acre, square meter, etc. You will then choose the blue Next button.

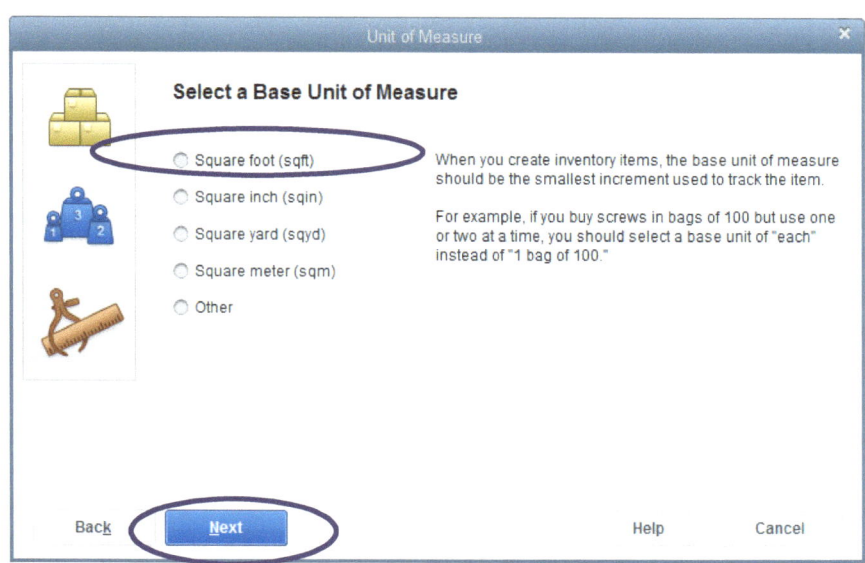

You will now need to choose from 5 different types of Base Unit of Measure. For our Carpenter, we will choose *Square foot*. You will then choose the blue Next button.

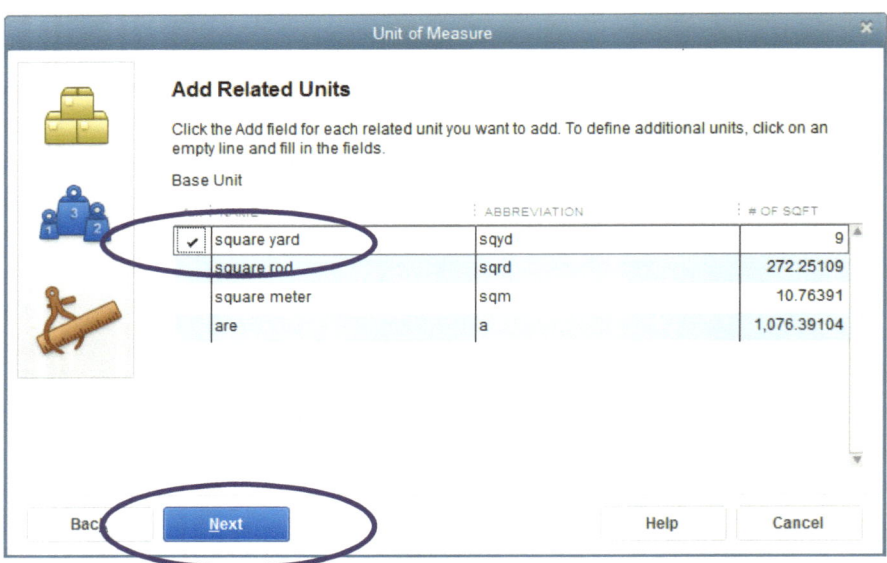

You now have the additional option adding related units but may not be required for your needs. In this example, we will choose Square Yard. You will then choose the blue Next button.

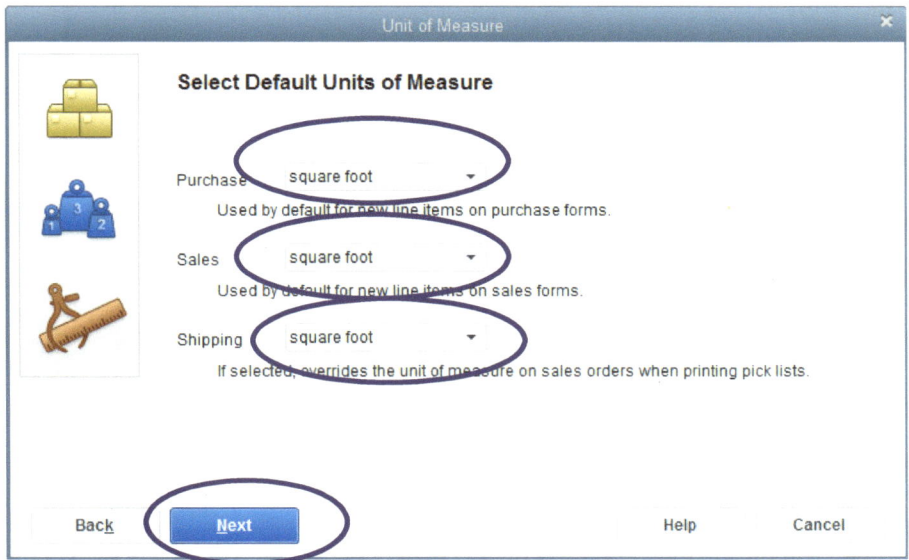

Select Default Units of Measure

Purchase   square foot ▾

    Used by default for new line items on purchase forms.

Sales   square foot ▾

    Used by default for new line items on sales forms.

Shipping   square foot ▾

    If selected, overrides the unit of measure on sales orders when printing pick lists.

Back   Next   Help   Cancel

You now have to *Select Default Units of* Measure based upon how you purchase the Item, how you sell the Item, and how you ship the Item. It is not a requirement that you choose all three to be the same unit of measurement, but you can only choose what's available from the drop-down menu. In this example, we will choose *square* foot for each choice. You will then choose the blue Next button.

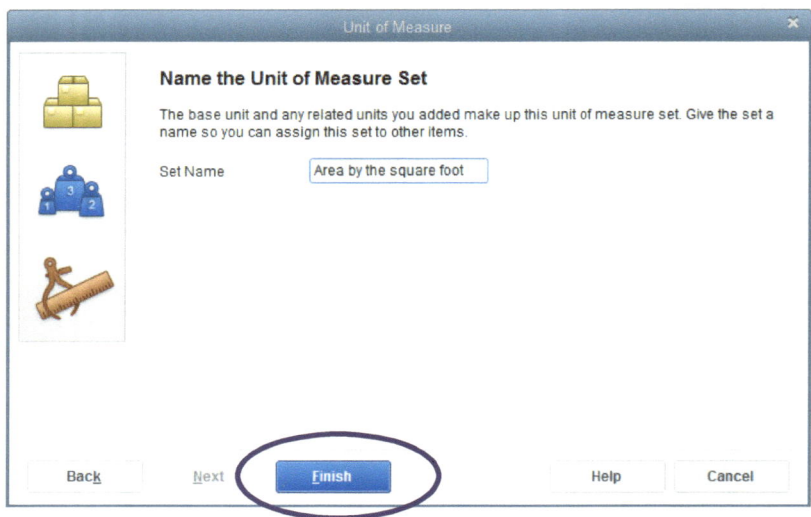

Upon setting your *Unit of Measure*, you must then *Name the Unit of Measure Set* and QuickBooks will automatically name it for you, however you have the option of changing it to another name. In this example, we will leave the information and choose the Finish button.

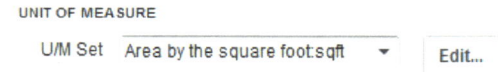

When completed, it will appear in the Carpenter Subitem as Area by the square foot:sqft.

Exercises

1. The following are Default Units of Measure except for:

    a. Count   b.   Length
    c. Size   d.   Volume

2. You can create a new Unit of Measurement not listed:

    a. True
    b. False

Objective 3: Performing searches and sorts in your Items List.

When you have a large number of items that you have set-up, it's easier to perform basic searches instead of trying to scroll through your Items List. You are also offered the option of performing sorts to find easier ways of looking for items in particular groups/categories.

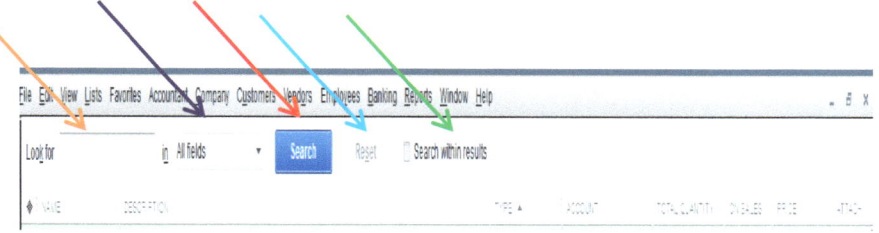

At the very top of your Items List, you'll see a box labeled as "Look for" that will allow you to type in a specific item name or description word(s). When you have completed this step, then you have the option of searching in "All fields" or from your drop-down menu, choose:

> Item Name/Number
> Description (Sales)
> Purchase Description
> Preferred Vendor
> Man. Part Number
> U/M
> U/M Set
> Custom Fields

When you've determined what you're looking for, choose the blue Search button. If you still need to "drill down" further, check the box "Search within results" to specifically look only what was provided in your original search.

For this example, we will see any Item with the word "custom" in it. QuickBooks will recognize the word only – not if it's upper or lower case. Then choose the Search button.

Upon finding the Item you want, choose the "Reset" button and the original Items List will return.

Sorting the List

When sorting your Items List, you will see a "diamond" shape above each column. You can sort each list by the column that is displayed, i.e. Name, Description, Type, Account, Total Quantity, On Sales Order, etc. To re-sort back to the original list, choose the diamond over the column you want to re-sort to.

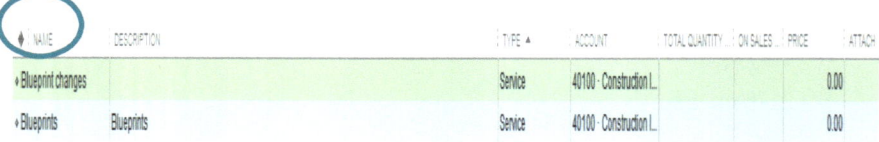

Search Within Results

If you need to further "drill down" into your results, as in the example used before with the word "custom," you can check the box "Search within results" with the word "top"; click the Search button.

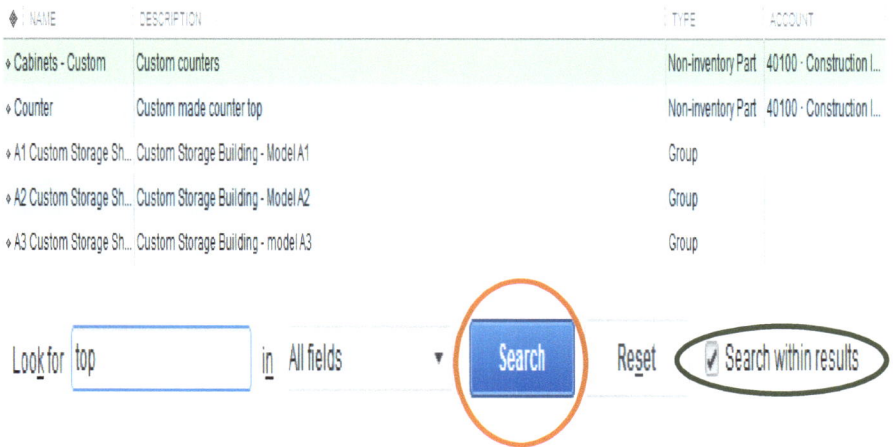

This therefore allows you to find only one item with the word "counter" in the Items List. Choose the Reset button again.

Exercises

1.   The Description section refers to the Expense or Sales side?

    a. Expense
    b. Sales

2.   The diamond allows you to resort your list:

    a. True
    b. False

Answer Key

<u>Objective 1</u>

1.   New

2.   Payment

3.   False

4.   True

5.   True

6.   True

7.   Inventory

<u>Objective 2</u>

1.   Size

2.   True

<u>Objective 3</u>

1.   Sales

2.   True

www.ingramcontent.com/pod-product-compliance
Lightning Source LLC
Chambersburg PA
CBHW040923180526
45159CB00002BA/590